Emoji Coloring Book

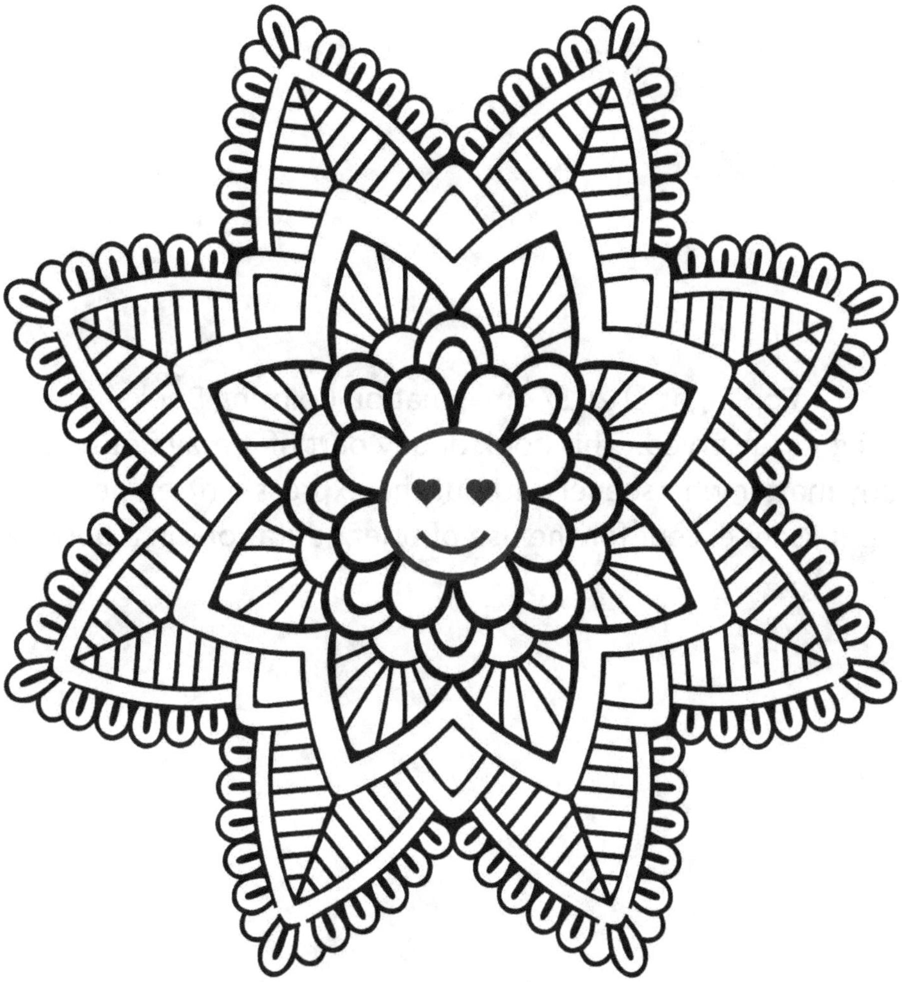

30 Cute Emoji Coloring Pages
For Stress Relief & Relaxation

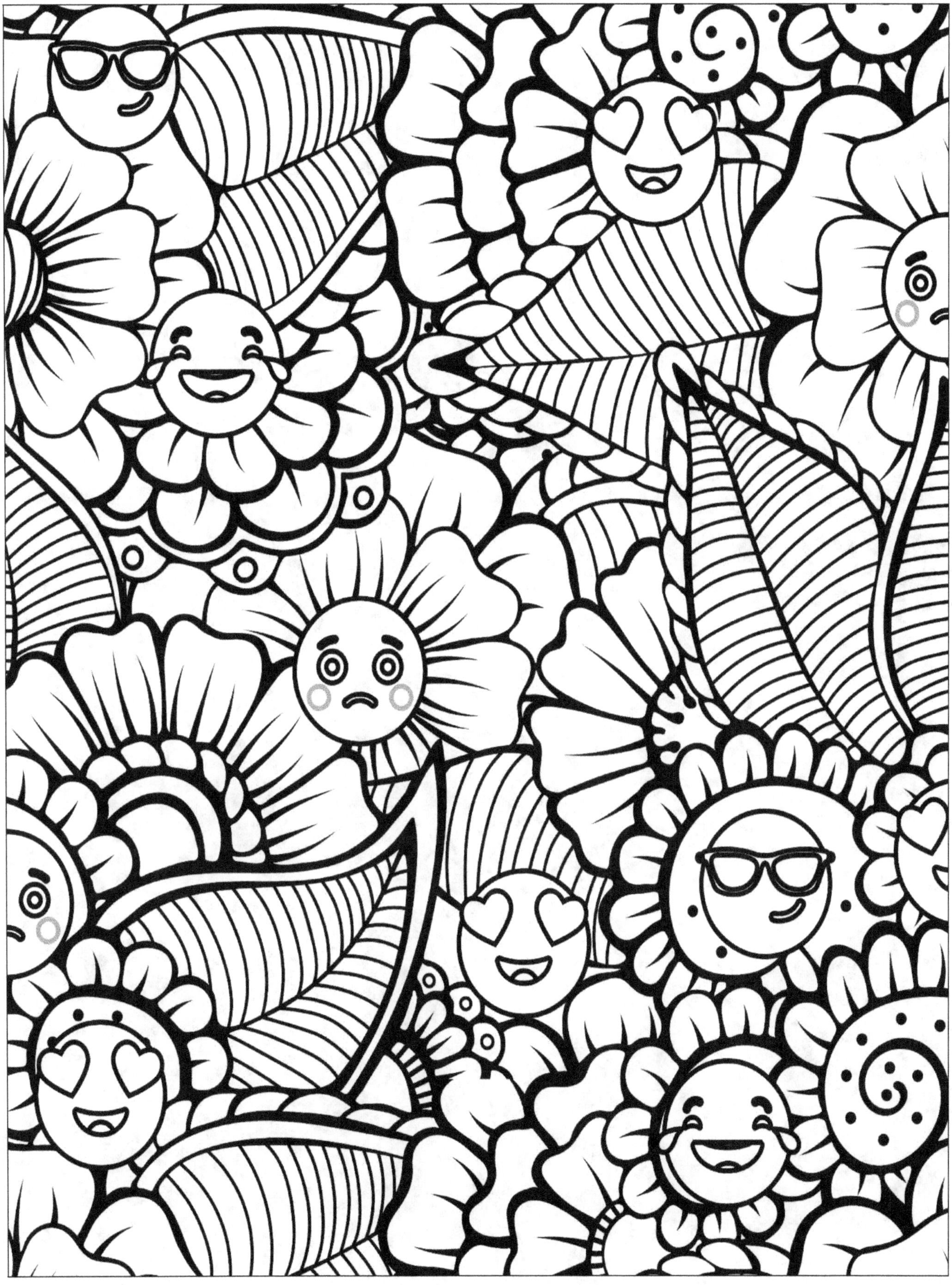

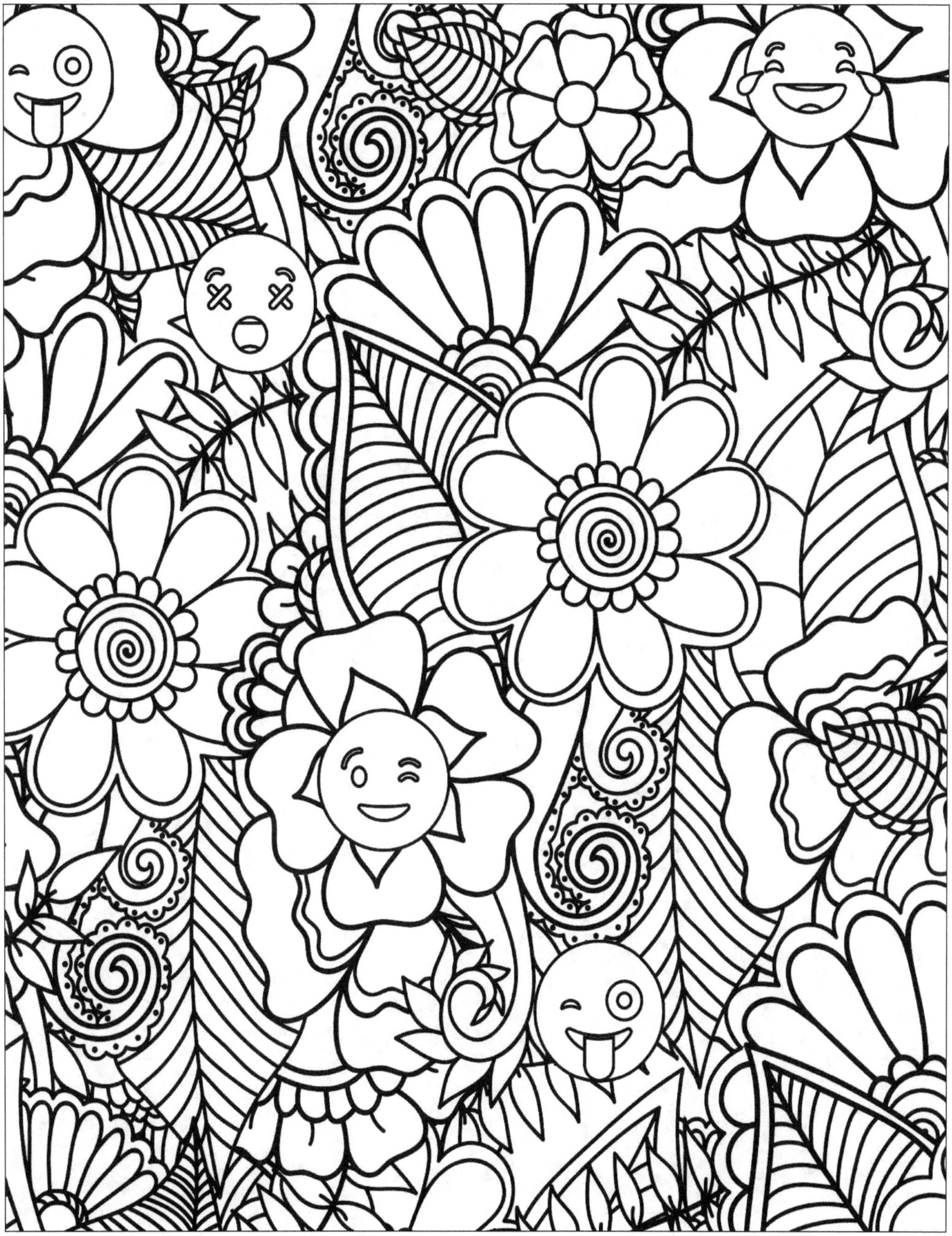

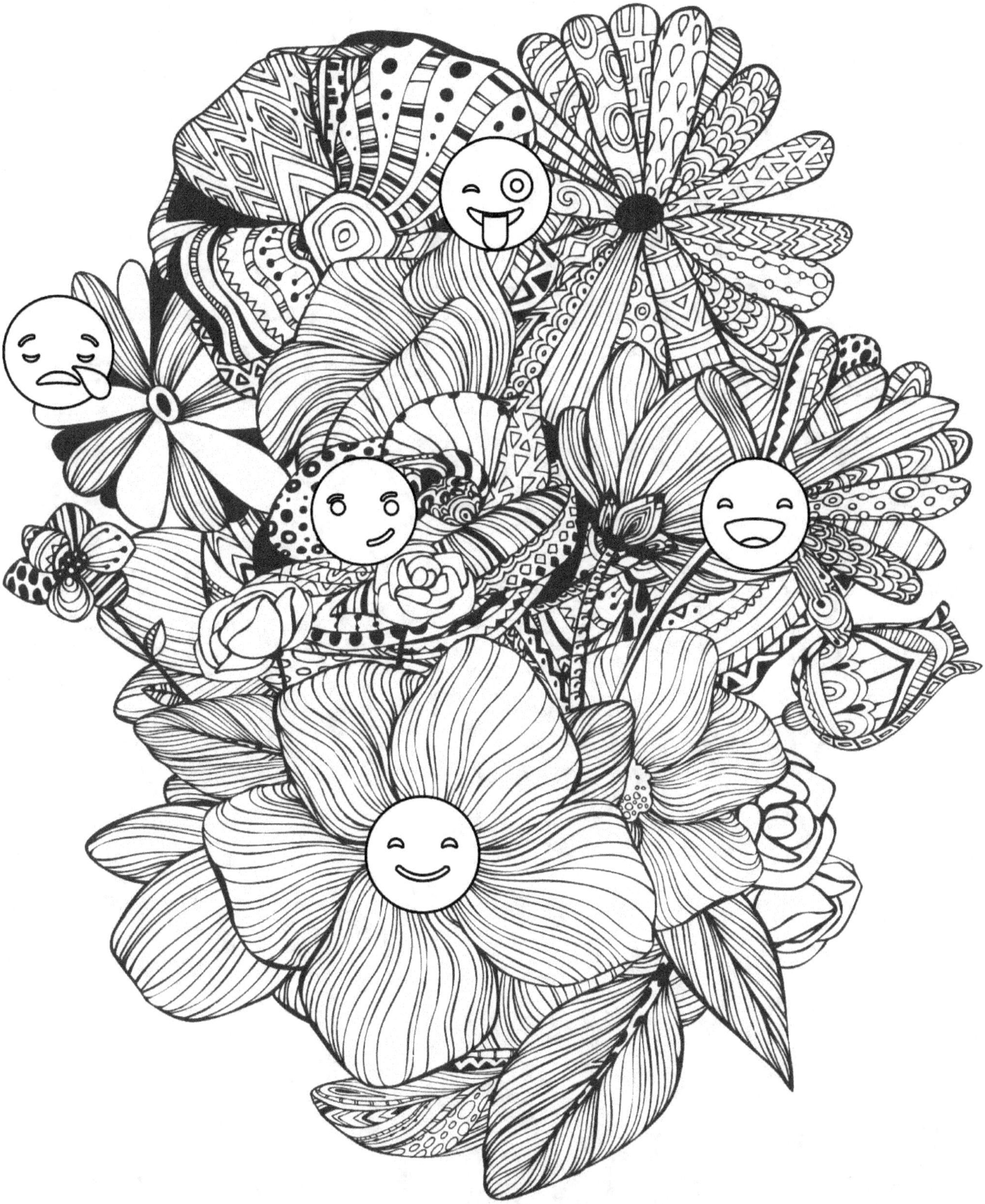

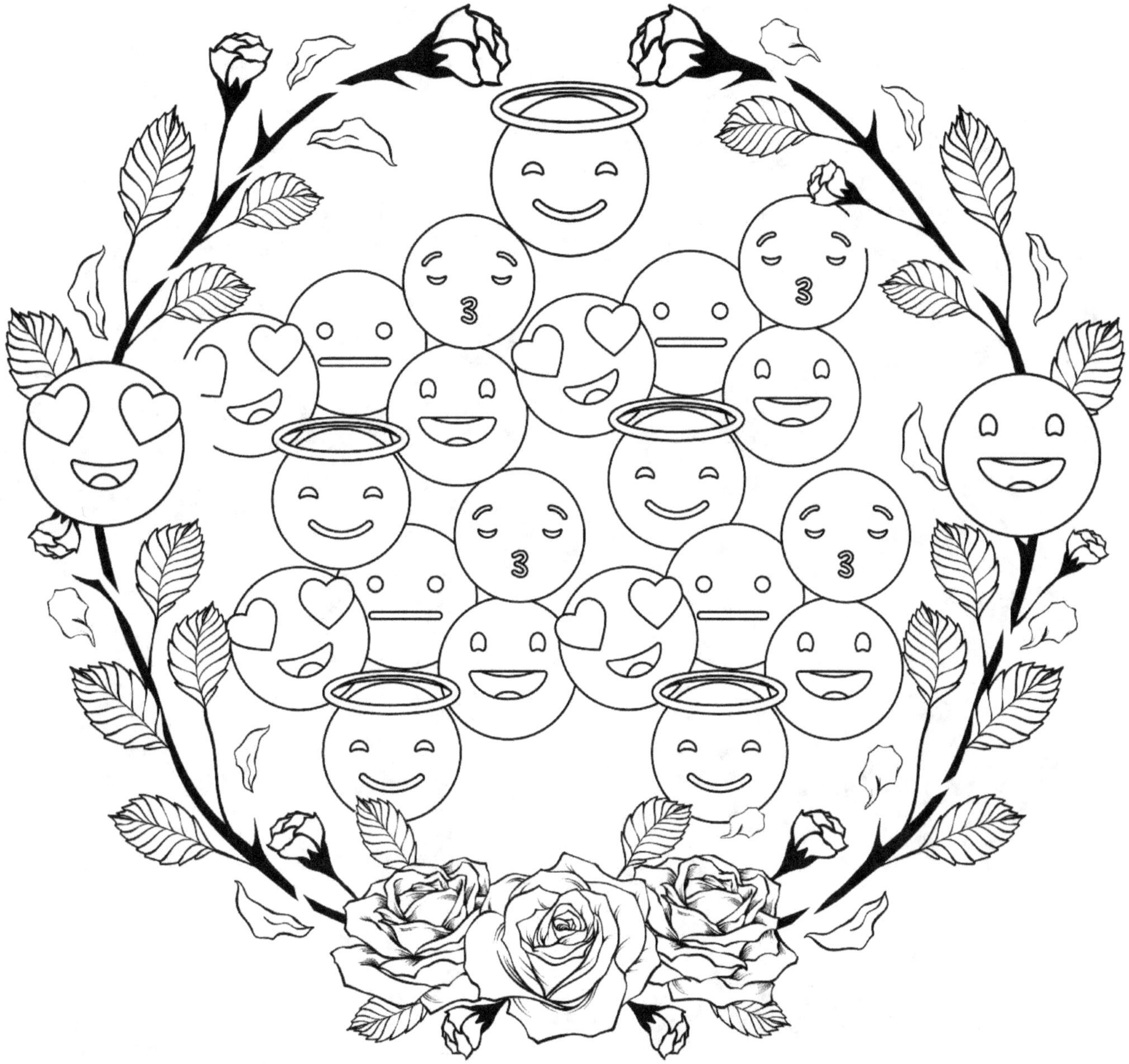

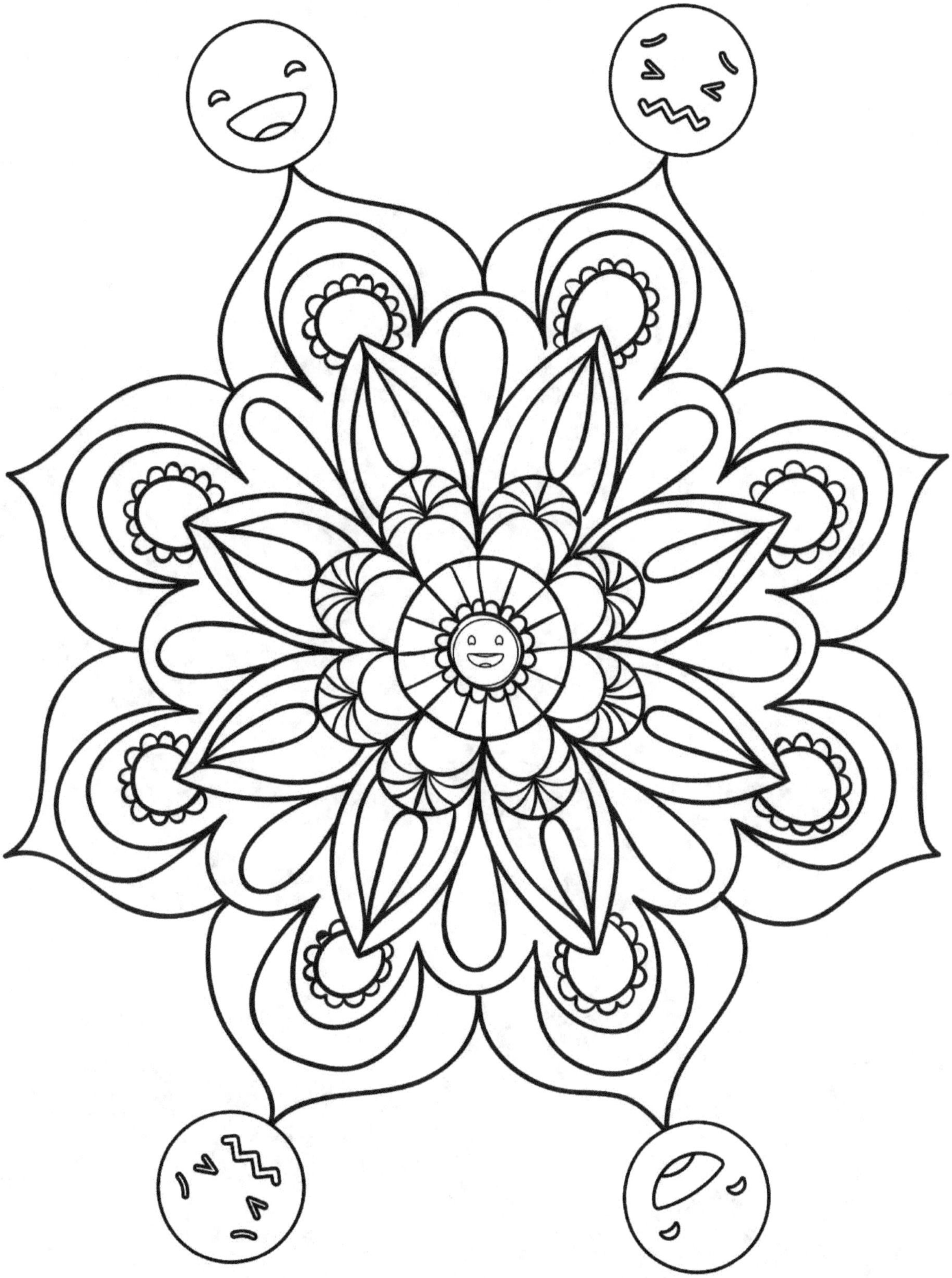

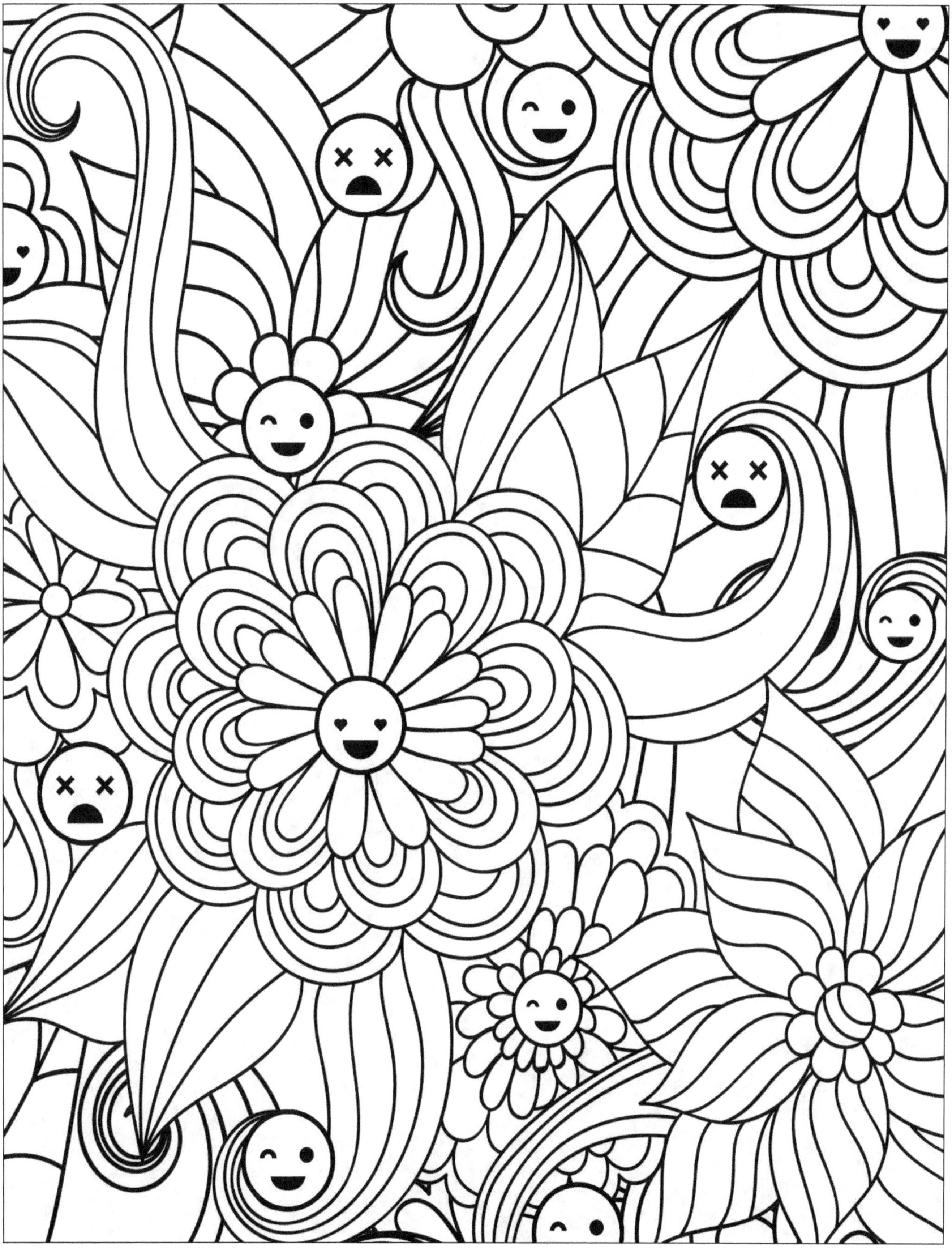

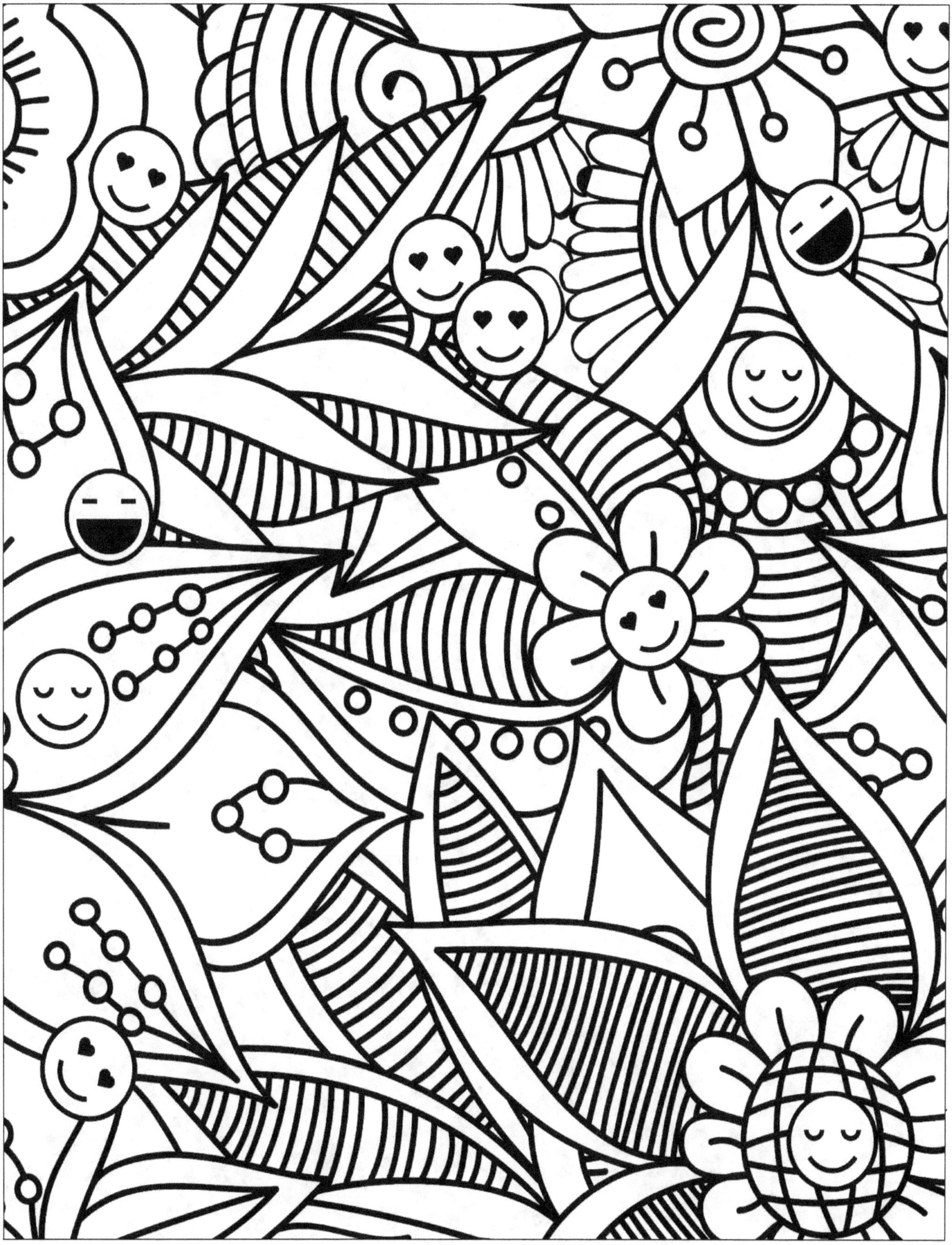

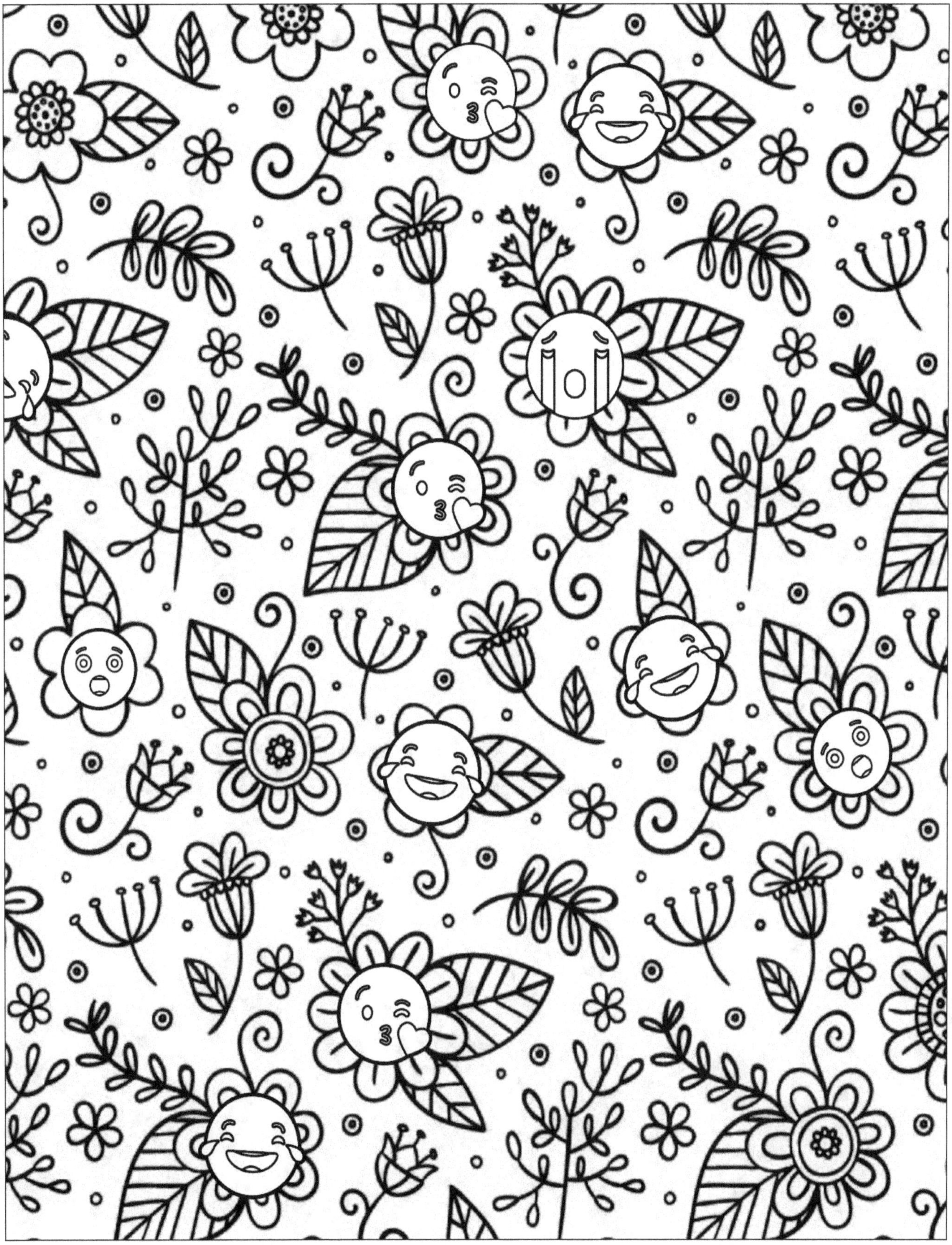

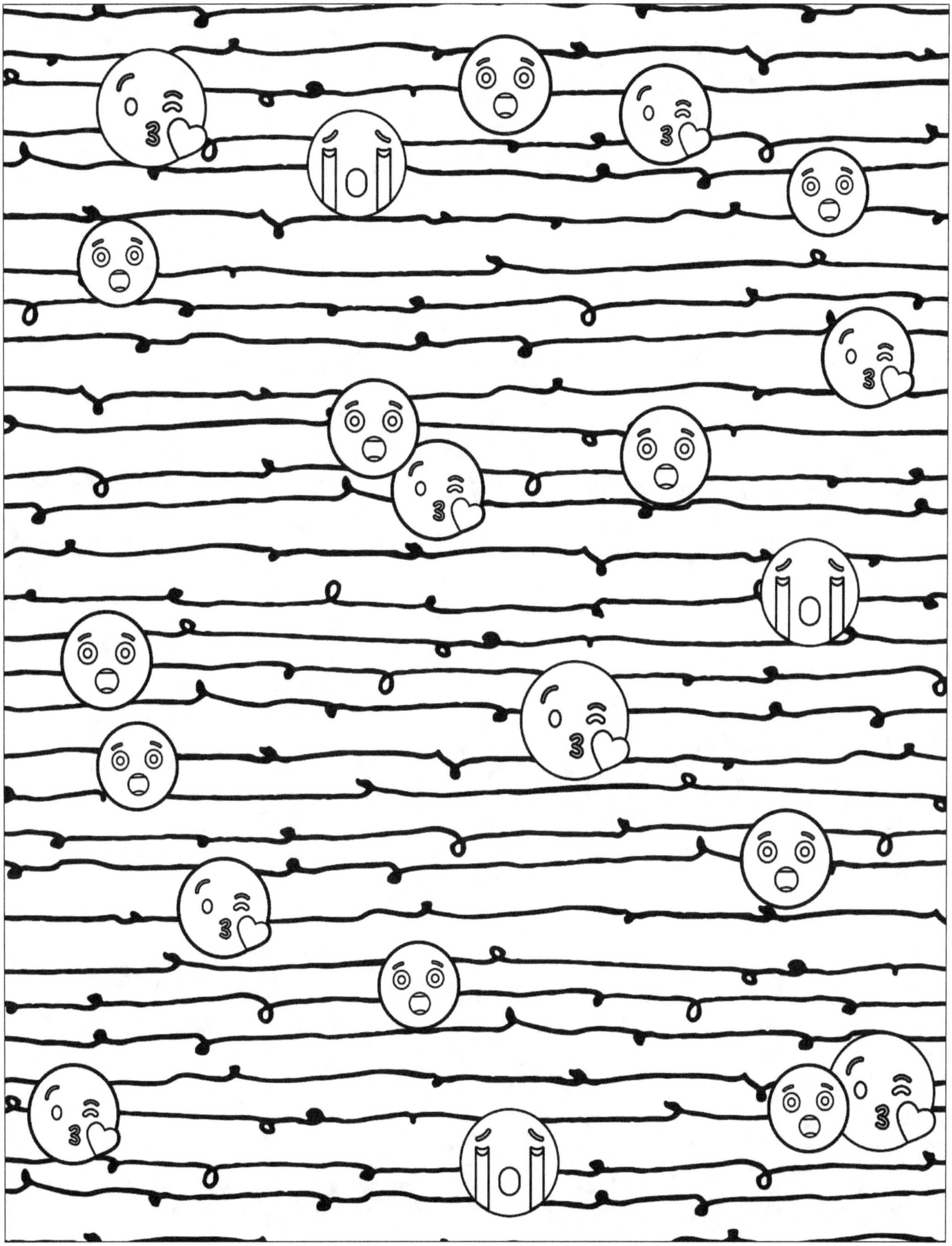

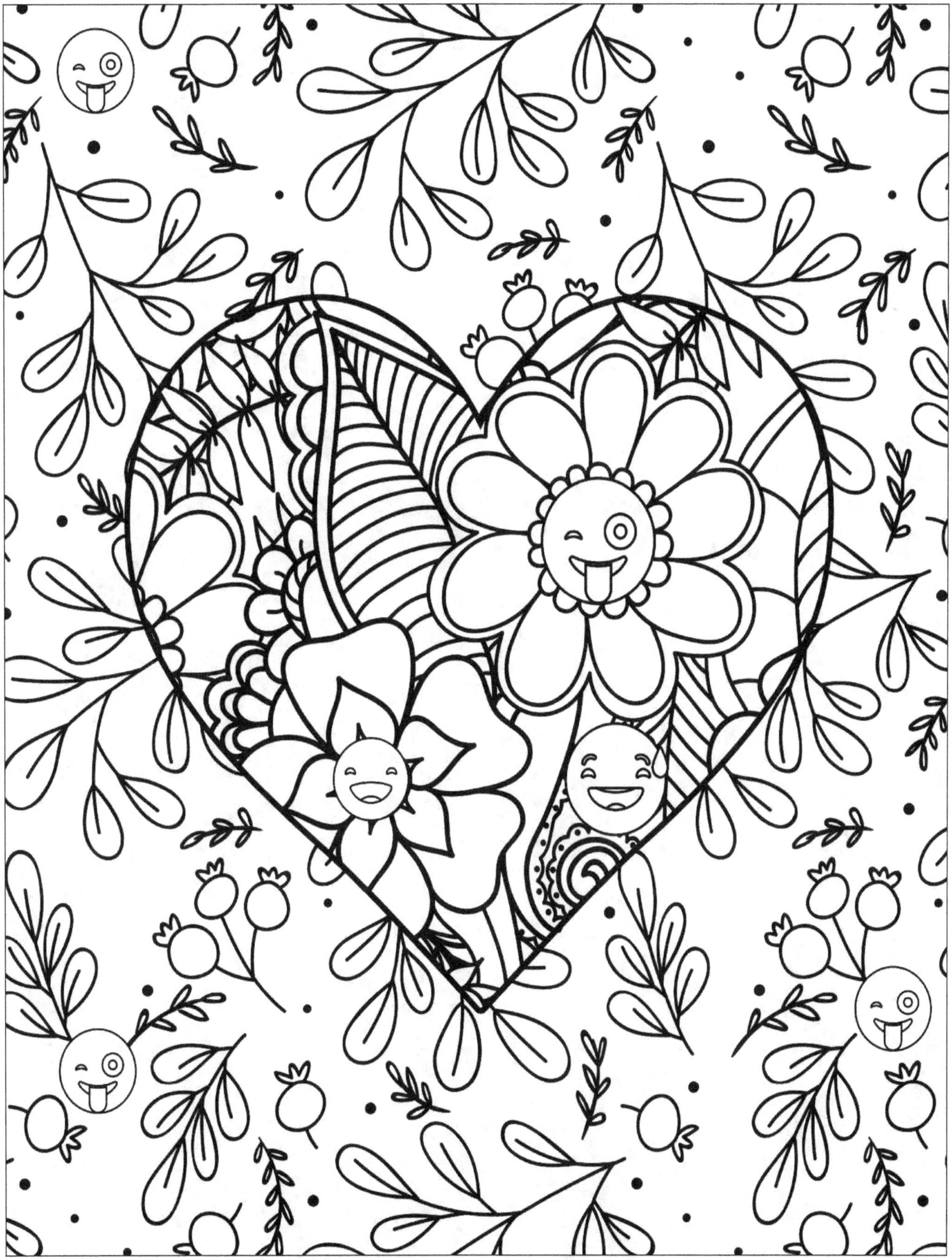

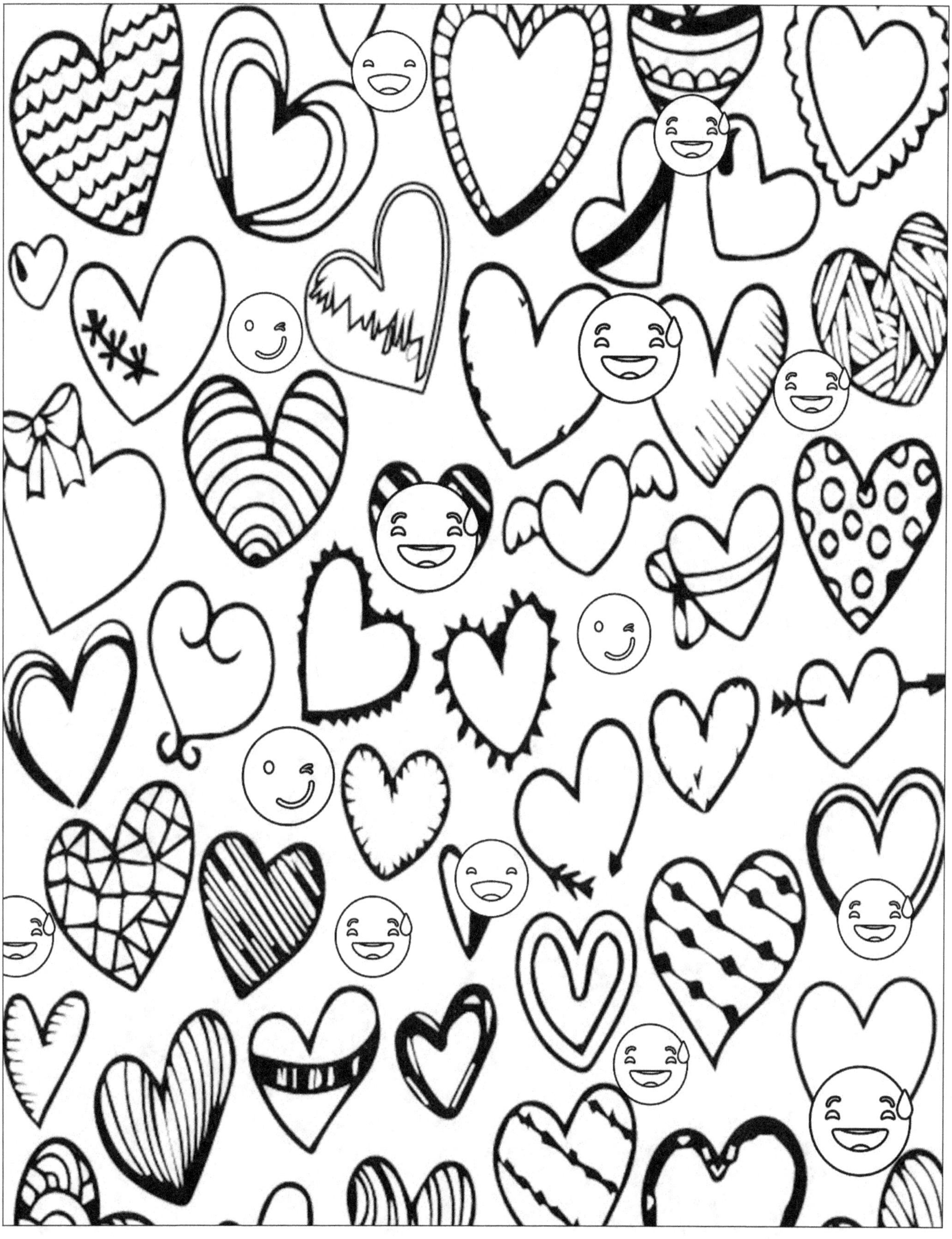

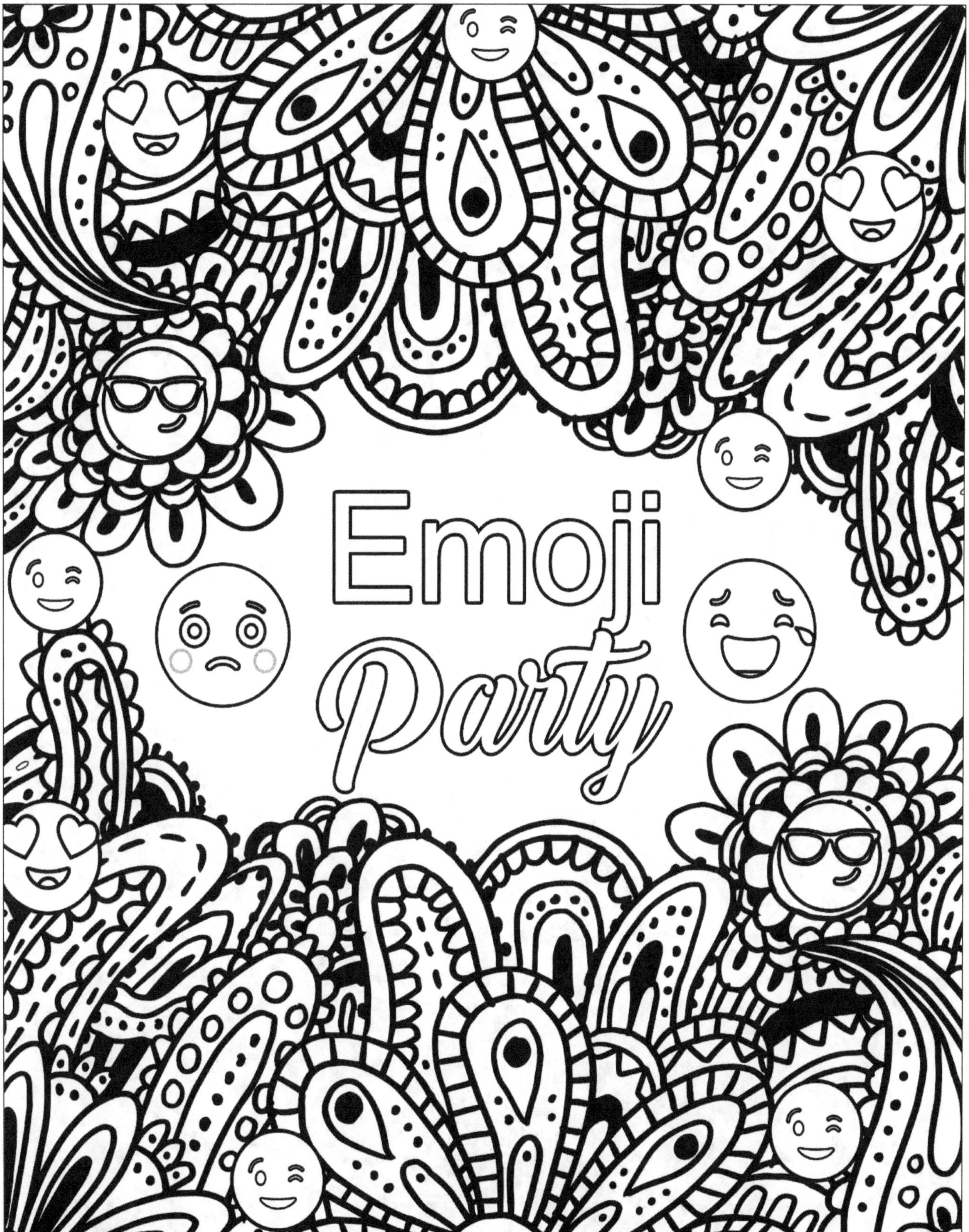
Emoji
Party

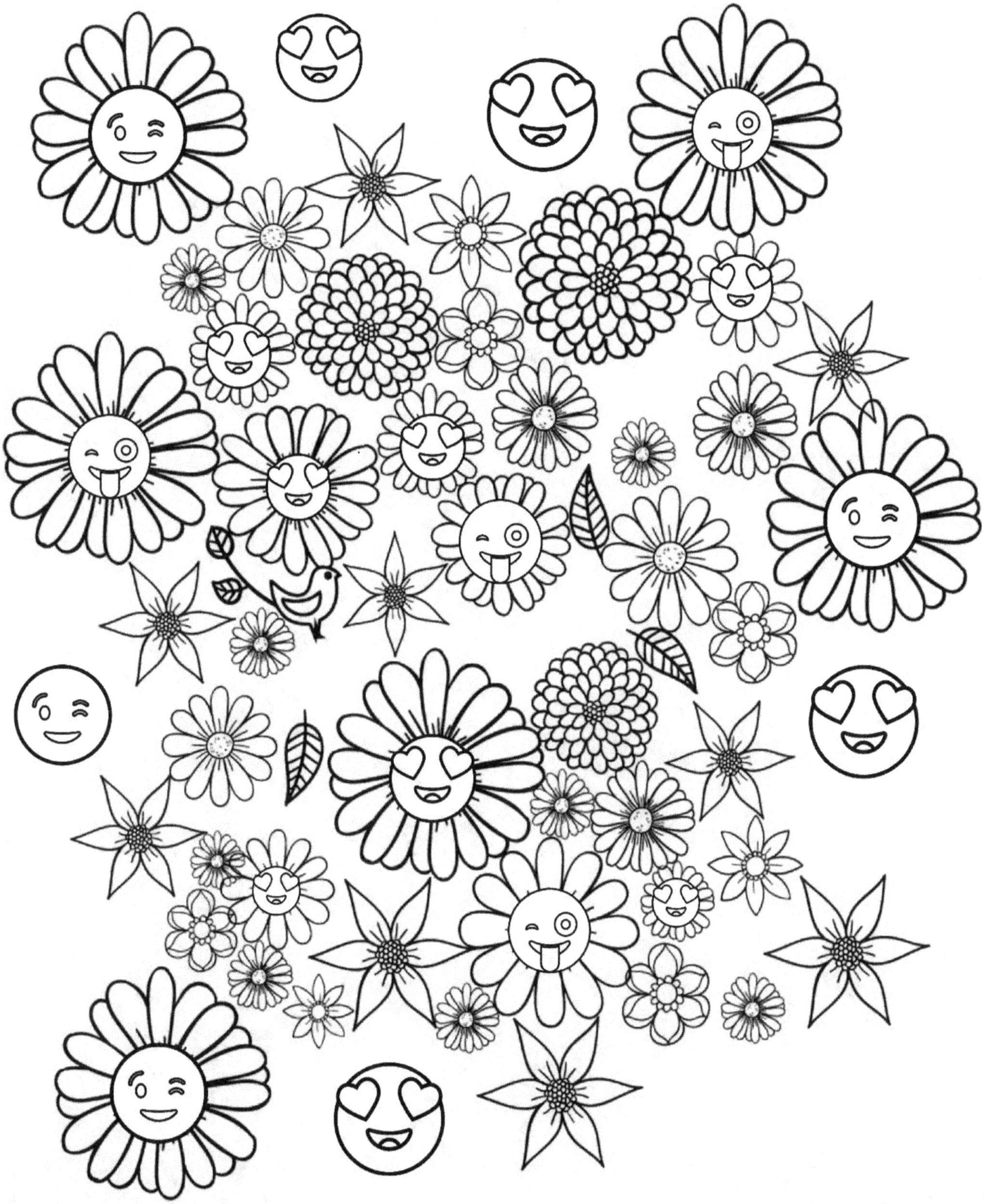

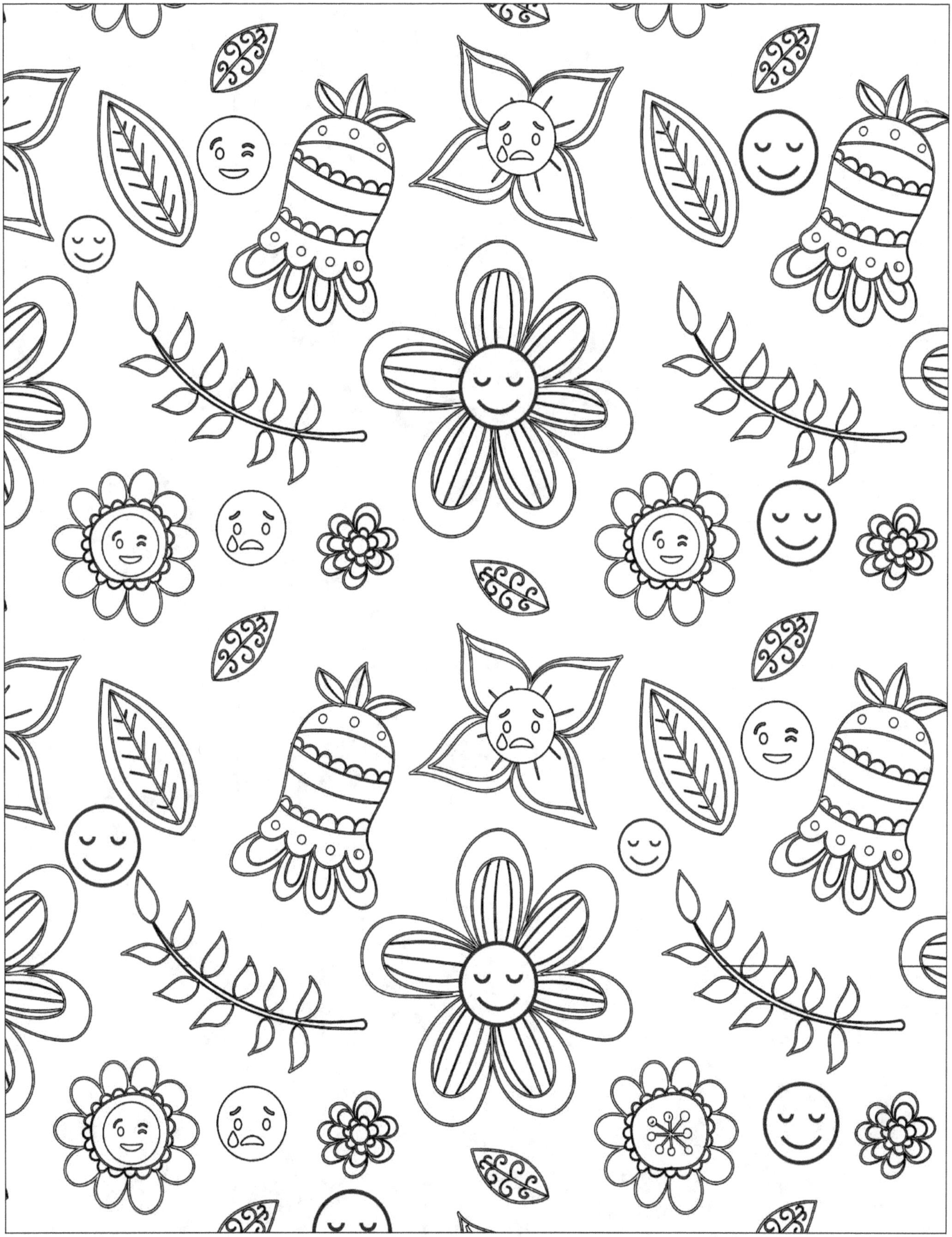

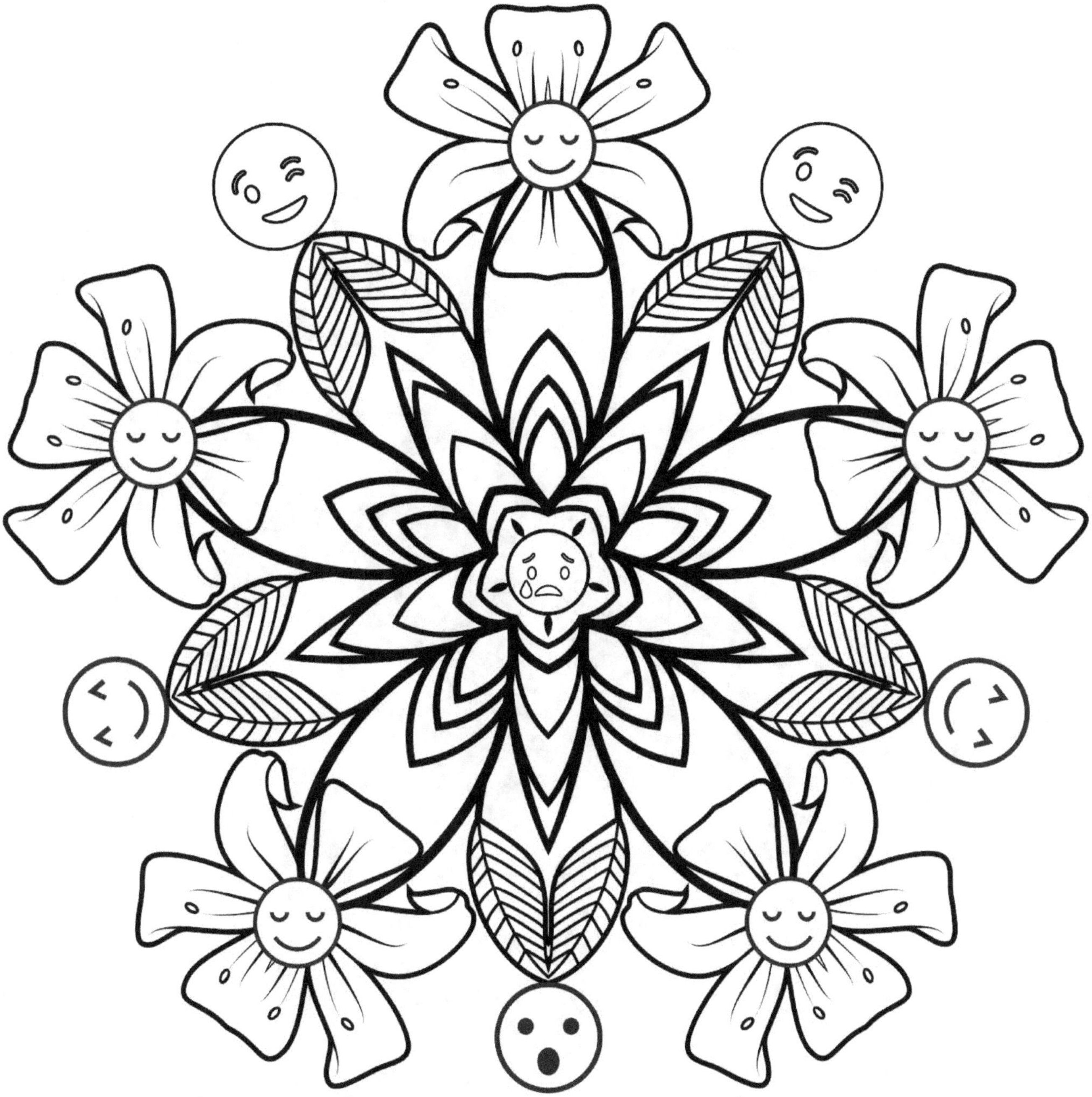

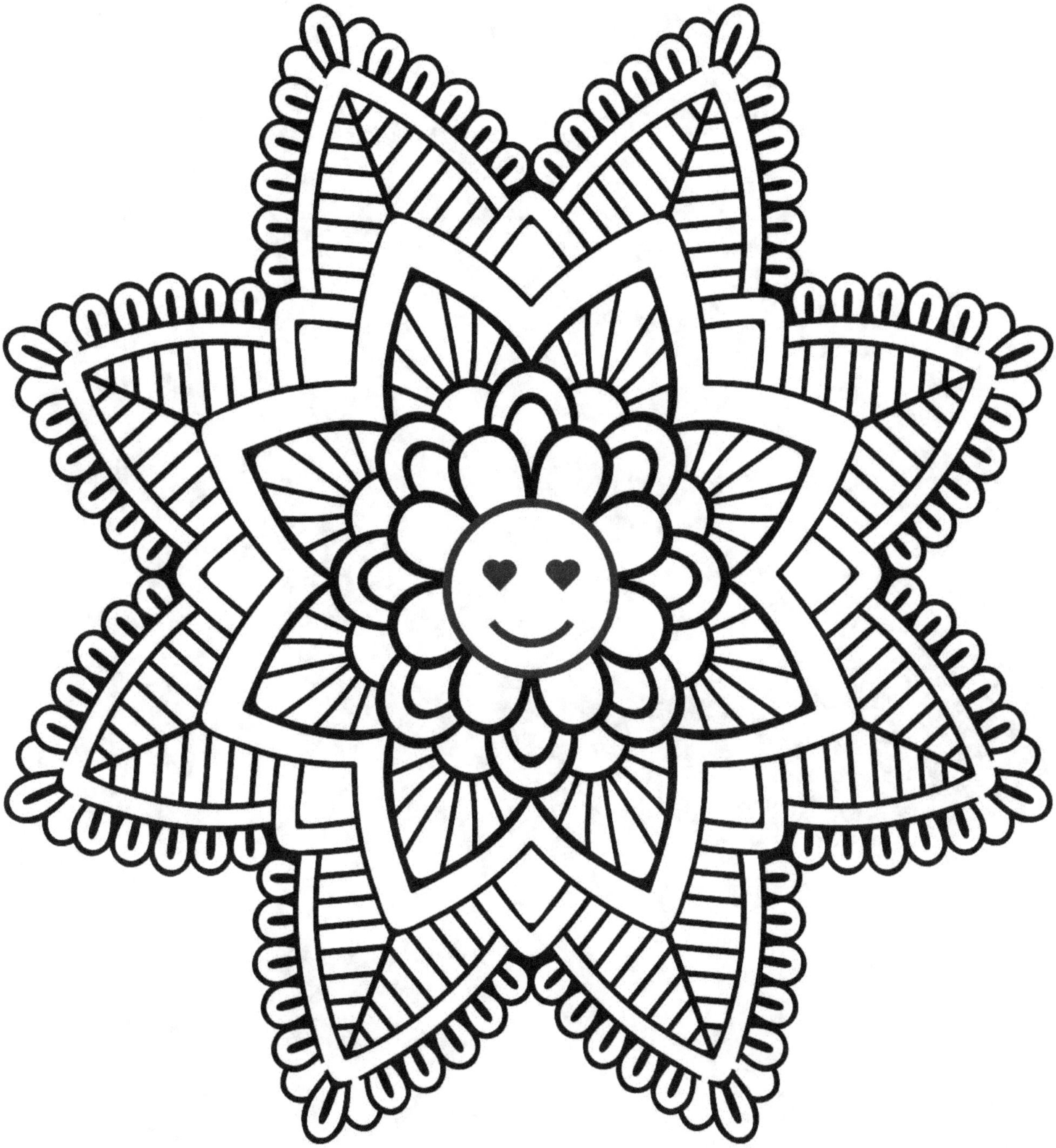

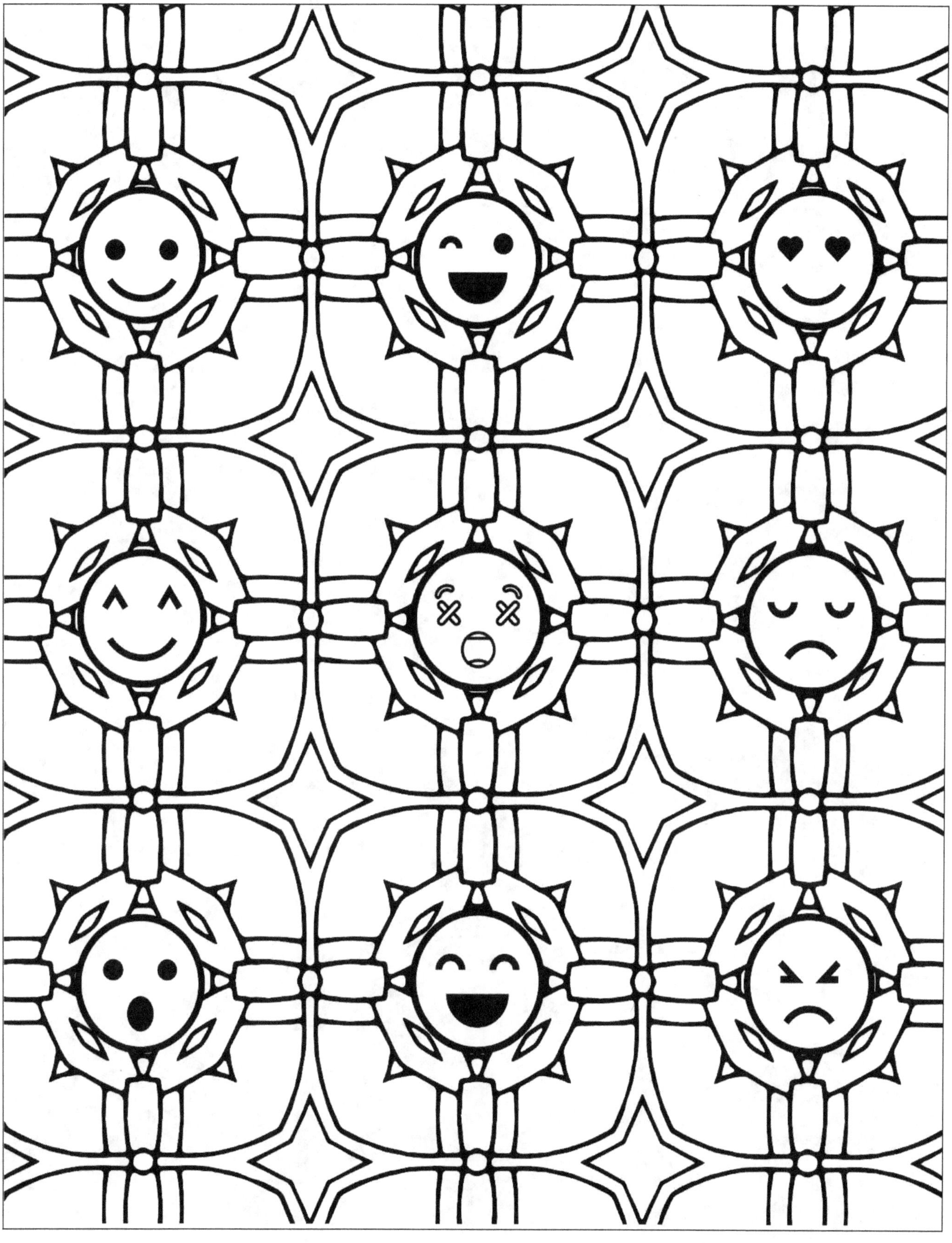

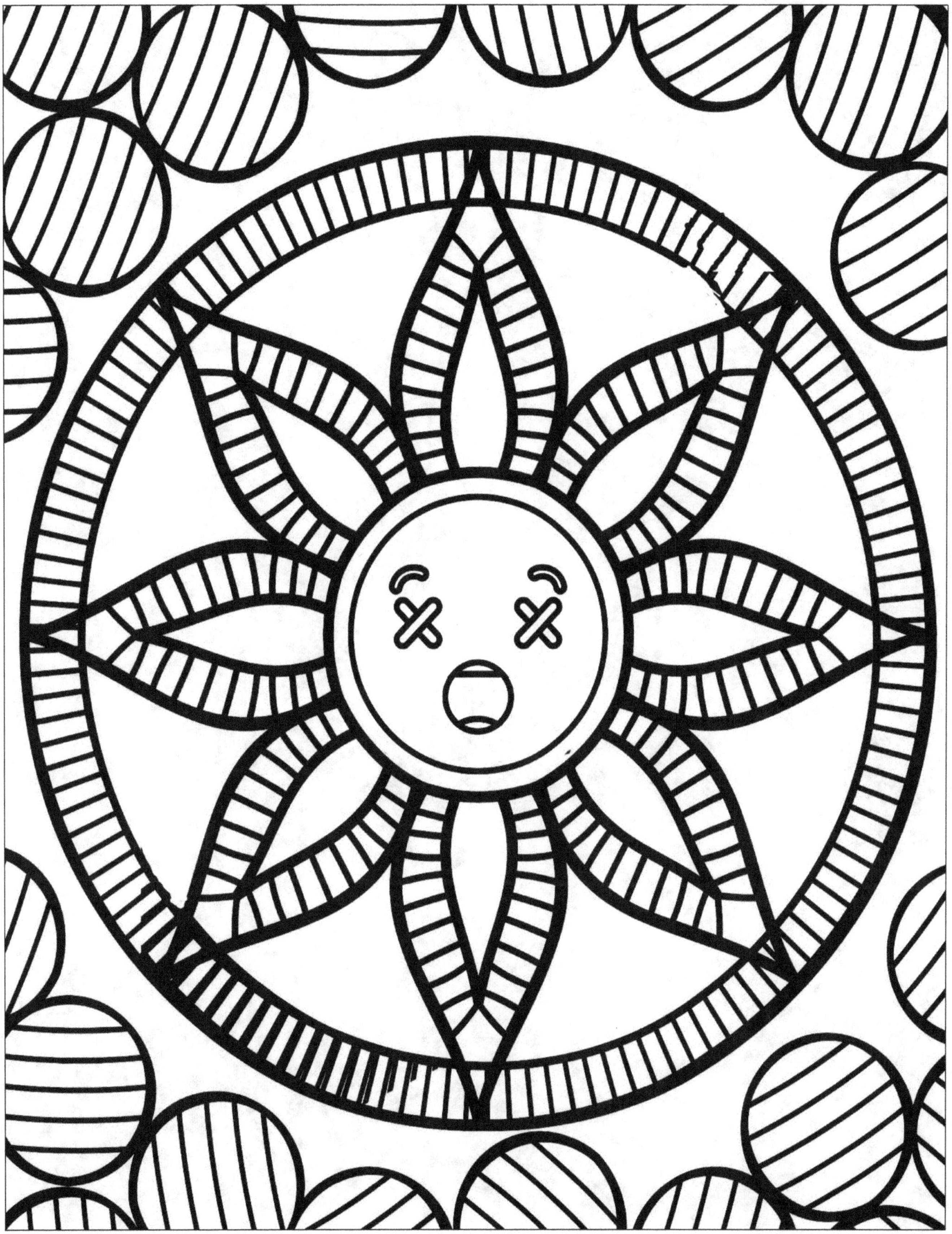

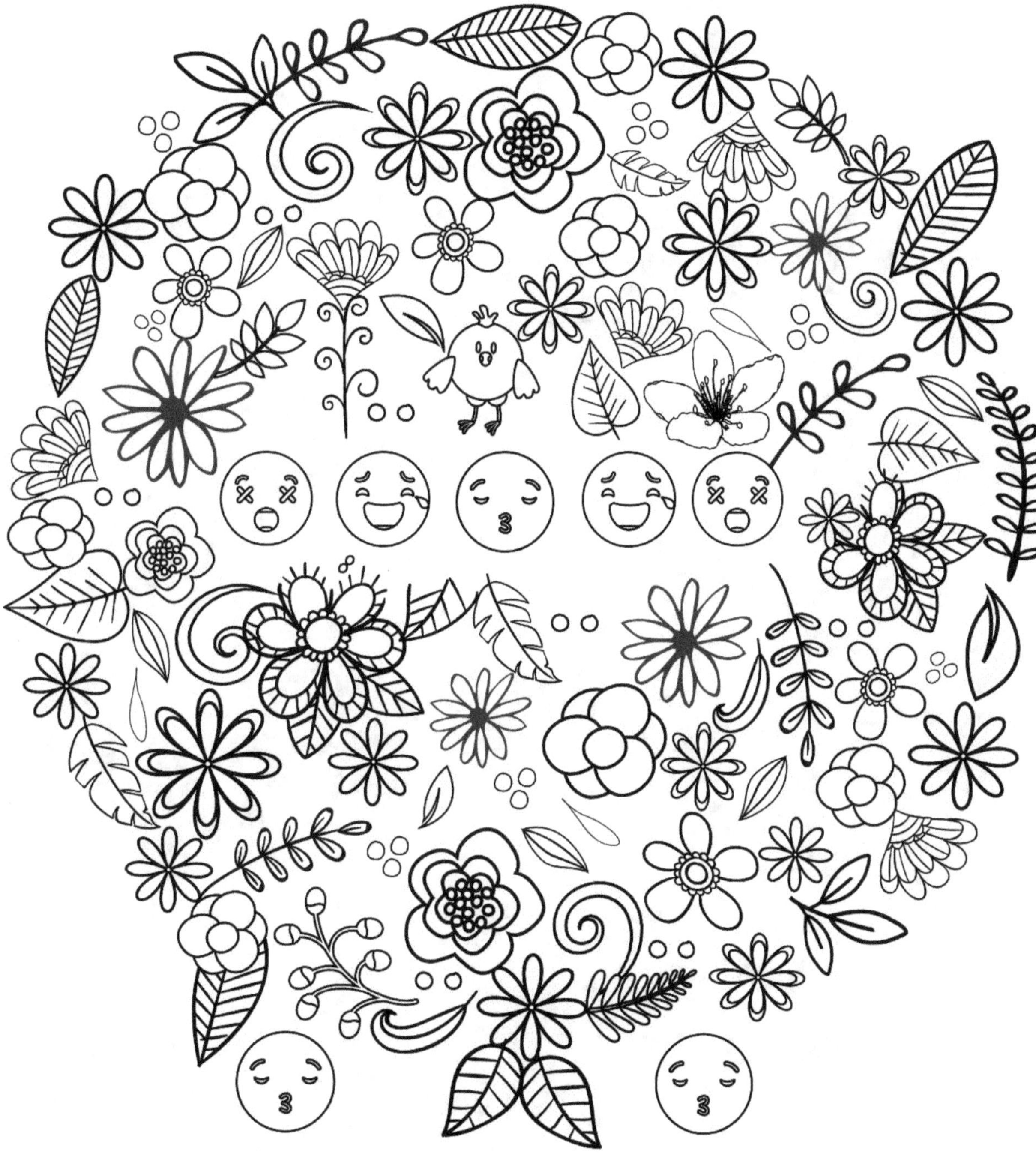

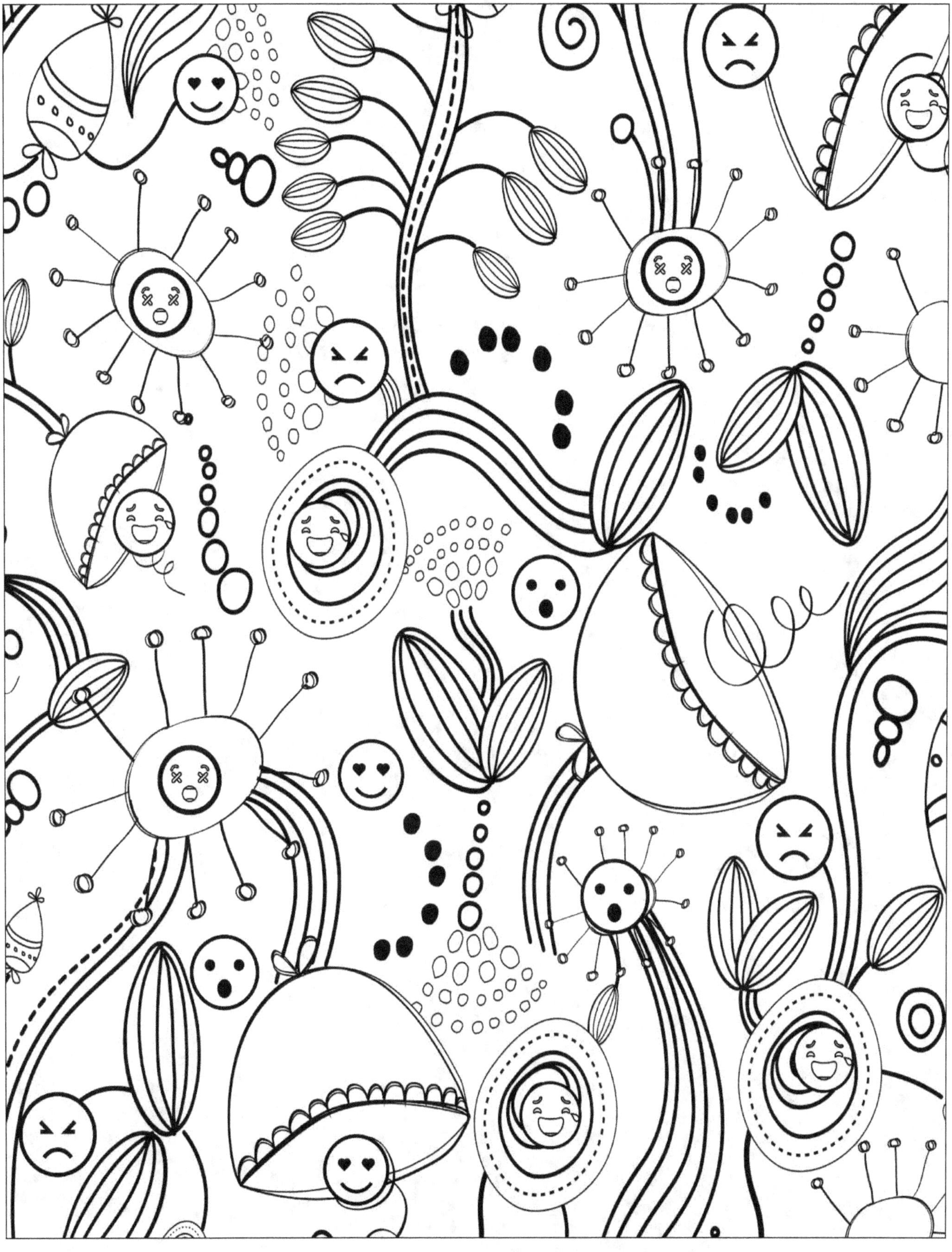

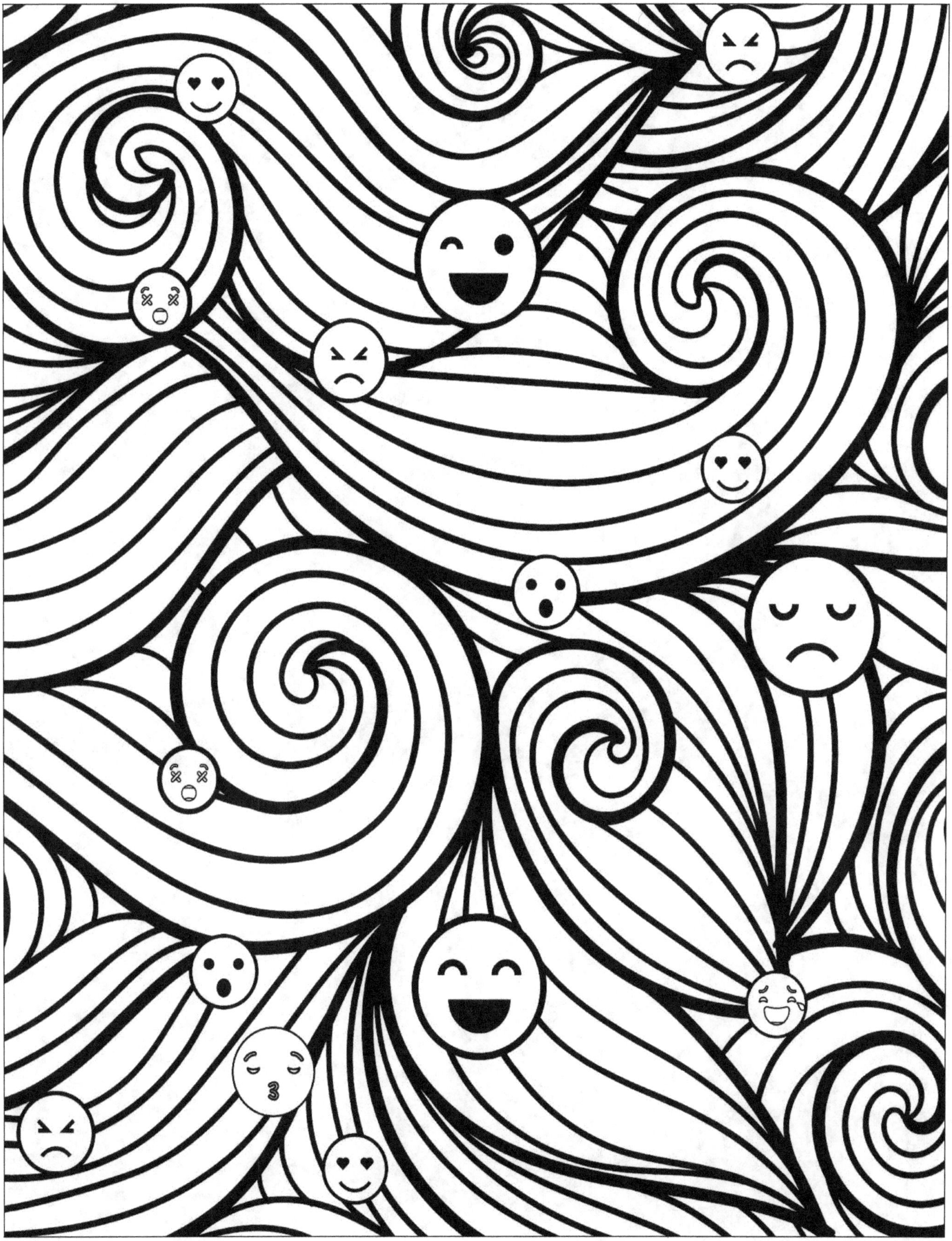

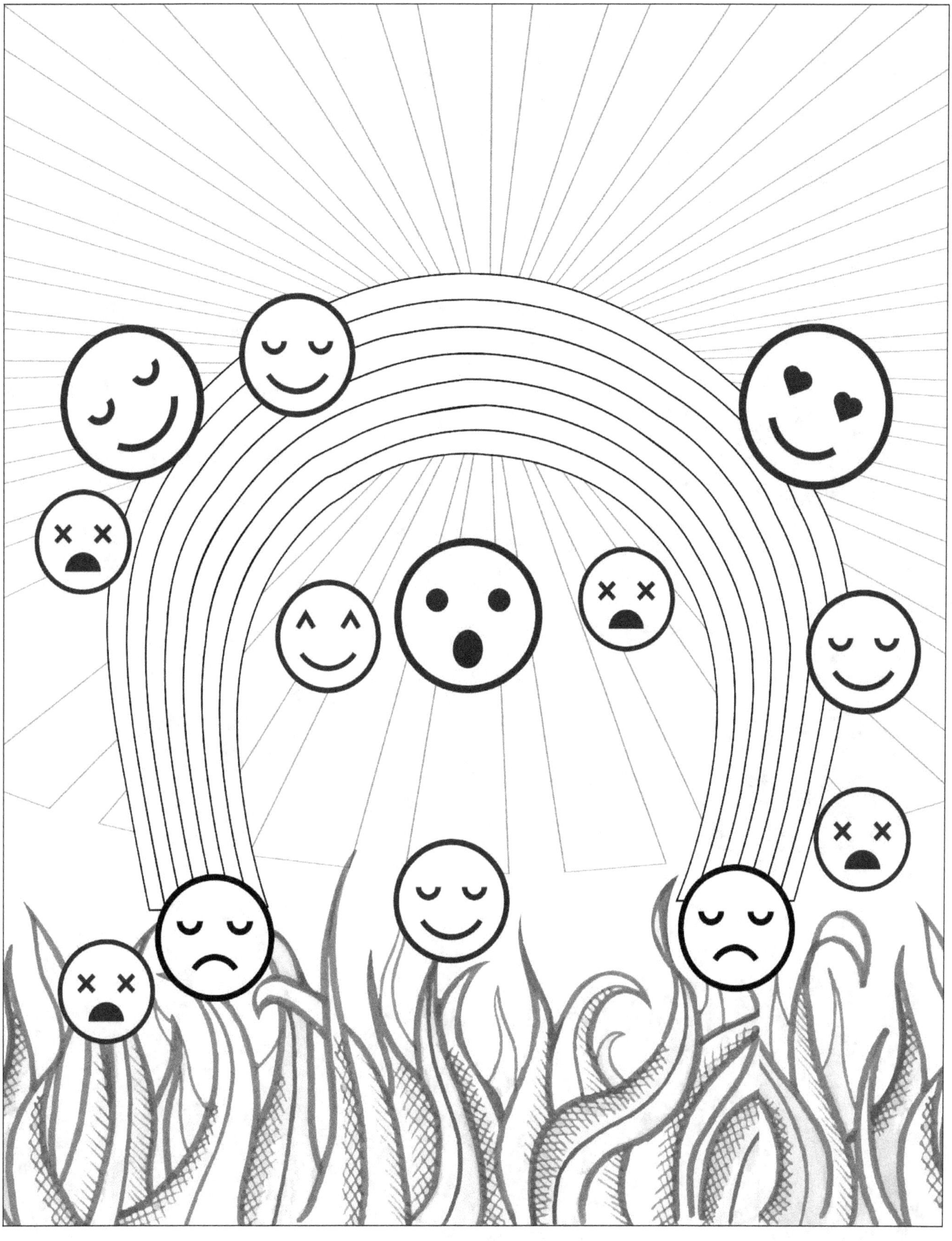

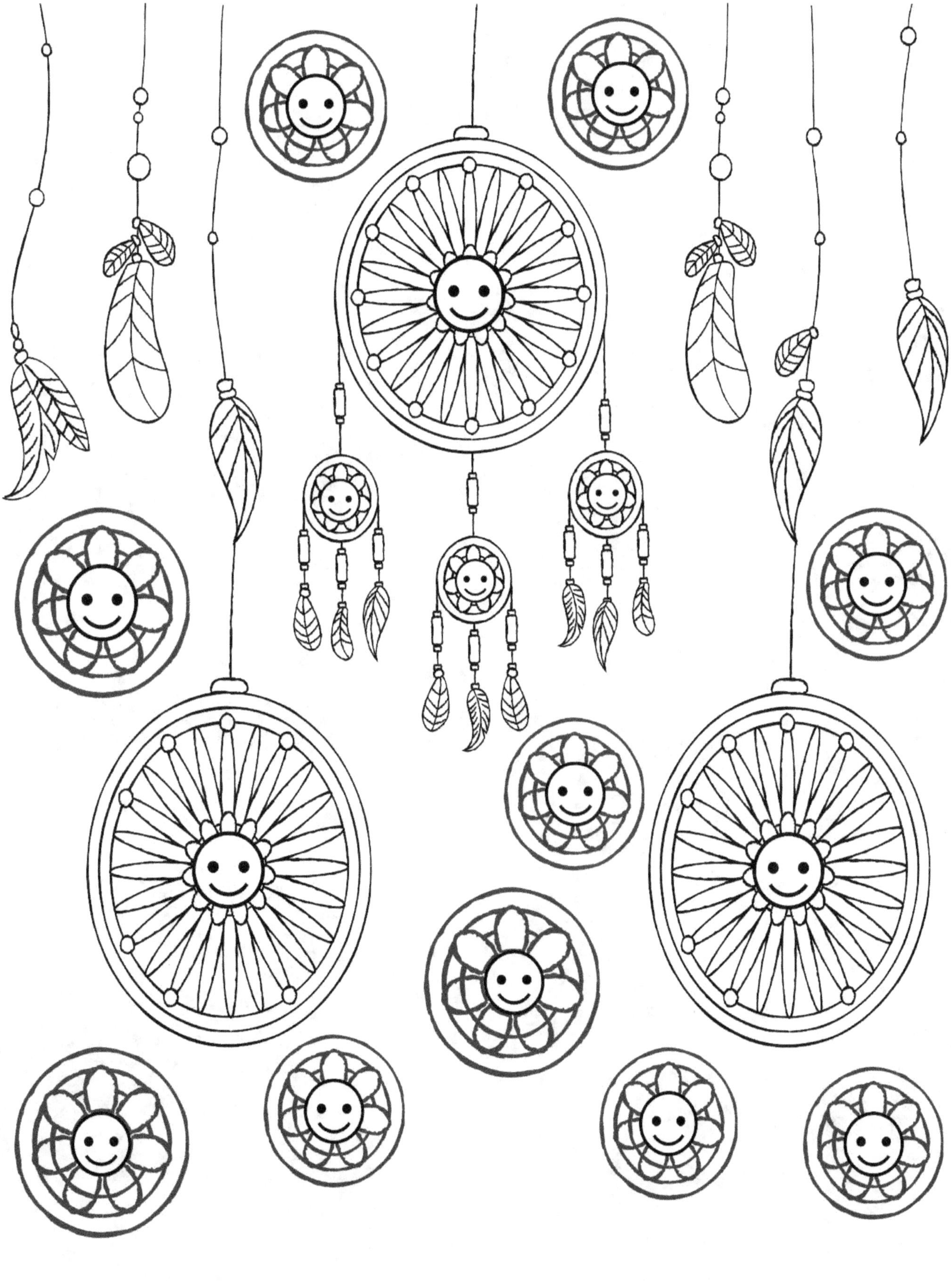

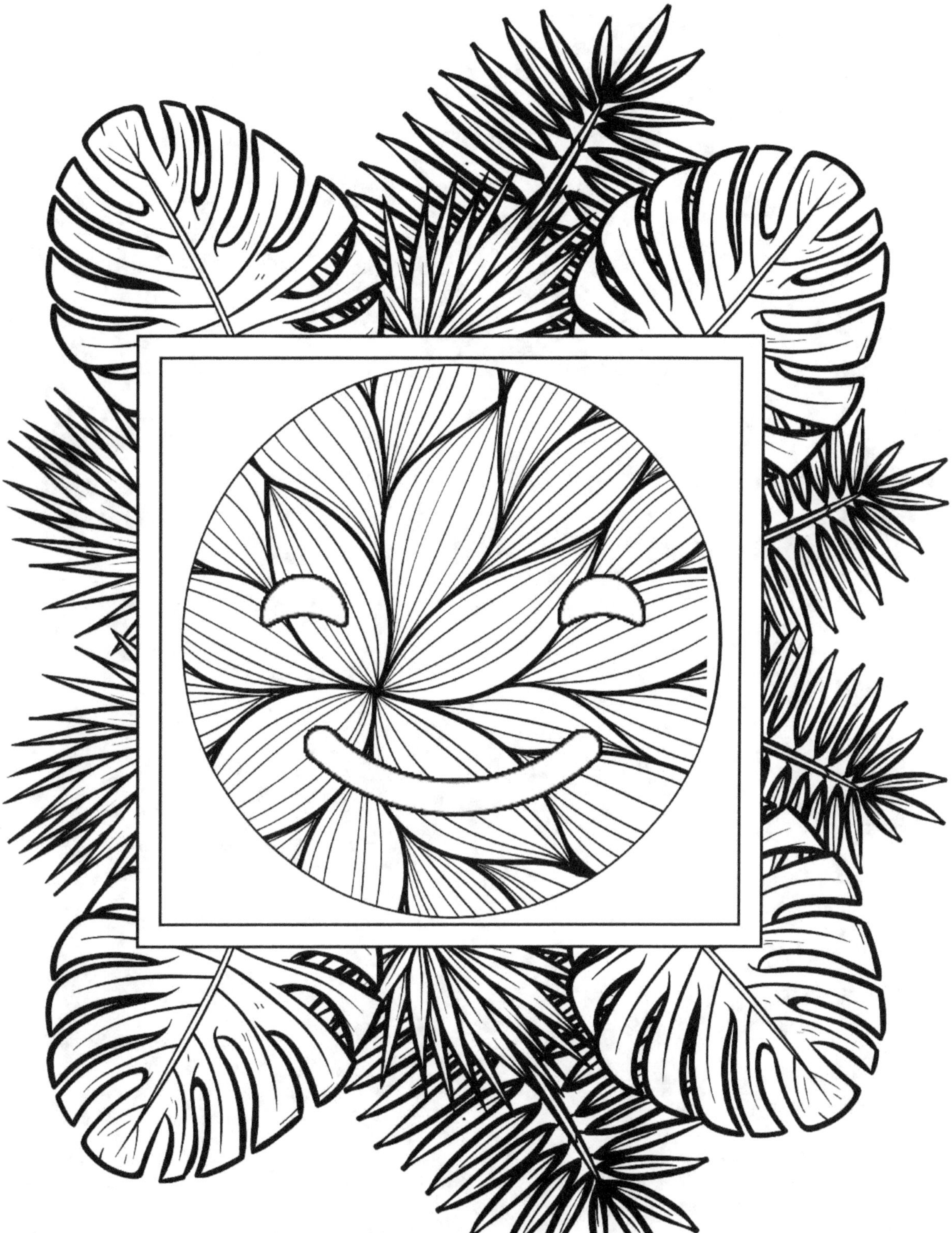

www.ingramcontent.com/pod-product-compliance
Lightning Source LLC
Chambersburg PA
CBHW081257180526
45170CB00007B/2460